WOMEN'S STORIES *from* HISTORY

Stories of Women in
WORLD
WAR II
We Can Do It!

Andrew Langley

heinemann
raintree

© 2015 Heinemann Raintree
an imprint of Capstone Global Library, LLC
Chicago, Illinois

To contact Capstone Global Library please call 800-747-4992, or visit our web site
www.capstonepub.com

Edited by Penny West
Designed by Philippa Jenkins
Original illustrations © Capstone Global Library Ltd 2015
Illustrated by Nigel Chilvers—Advocate Art
Picture research by Tracy Cummins
Production by Helen McCreath
Originated by Capstone Global Library Ltd
Printed and bound in China by Leo Paper Group

18 17 16 15 14
10 9 8 7 6 5 4 3 2 1

Library of Congress Cataloging-in-Publication Data
Langley, Andrew, 1949-
  Stories of women in World War II : we can do it! / Andrew Langley.
     pages cm—(Women's stories from history)
  Includes bibliographical references and index.
  ISBN 978-1-4846-0865-4 (hbk.)—ISBN 978-1-4846-0870-8 (pbk.)—ISBN 978-1-4846-0880-7
(ebook) 1. World War, 1939-1945—Women—Juvenile literature. 2. World War, 1939-1945—
Participation, Female—Juvenile literature. 3. Women—History—20th century—Juvenile
literature. I. Title.

  D810.W7L35 2015
  940.53092'520973—dc23   2014015508

This book has been officially leveled by using the F&P Text Level Gradient™ Leveling System.

Acknowledgments
We would like to thank the following for permission to reproduce photographs and artwork:
Alamy: © War Archive, 98; Capstone: Advocate Art/Nigel Chilvers, 6, 14, 23, 30, 39, 50, 52, 63,
74, 84, 95; Getty Images: George W. Hales, 4, Planet News Archive/SSPL, Cover; Imperial War
Museum: 69.

Every effort has been made to contact copyright holders of material reproduced in
this book. Any omissions will be rectified in subsequent printings if notice is given
to the publisher.

007186LEOS15

Contents

Introduction

In September 1939, German troops invaded Poland. Soon afterward, the United Kingdom and France declared war on Germany. World War II had begun. The fighting spread across the globe, drawing in many other nations, including the Soviet Union and the United States (as allies of the United Kingdom and France), and Italy and Japan (on the German side). More than 75 million people fought in the war—nearly all of them men.

This left a huge gap in the workforce. Who was going to produce the weapons and food and do many other important jobs? The answer was women. Millions took on work that they had rarely done before, such as operating factory machines, driving ambulances, fighting fires, flying bombers, plowing fields, and cracking codes. A few became famous names. This book tells the true stories of four of these women.

Anne-Marie Walters:
Secret Agent

Anne-Marie Walters worked behind enemy lines in France. For seven months during World War II, she was a messenger for French Resistance groups, which were fighting back in secret against the occupying Germans. Anne-Marie was in constant danger of being captured, but her courage and quick thinking helped her survive.

Anne-Marie was born in 1923. Her father was English and her mother was French. The Walters family lived in the city of Geneva, Switzerland. Life there was good. The family went skiing in the winter and spent summer vacations on the sunny beaches of the south of France. Anne-Marie grew up speaking both English and French.

This happy period ended with the outbreak of World War II. In May 1940, as German forces prepared to invade France, the family left Switzerland and moved to the United Kingdom. Anne-Marie was determined to be a part of the struggle against the Nazis. Though her mother tried to stop her, she joined the Women's Auxiliary Air Force (WAAF) in 1941. This all-female service took on many of the daily jobs in Britain's Royal Air Force, leaving the men free to fight on the front line.

Anne-Marie began work near London as a plotter, tracking the positions of enemy aircraft over the United Kingdom. Little did she know that she would soon be heading for the front line herself. In July 1943, Anne-Marie was asked to join the Special Operations Executive (SOE). This top-secret band of men and women helped organize Resistance groups in countries occupied by the Germans.

The groups gathered important information about the German forces, which was sent back to London. They also caused as much damage as they could, including wrecking railroads and weapons factories and arranging escape routes for airmen who were shot down. To support them, British planes dropped supplies of arms, radio equipment, money, and other essential items into France.

Why was Anne-Marie invited to join a secret and very dangerous organization like the SOE? For a start, she could speak French perfectly. The Germans would think she was just another French citizen. The other reason was that she was a woman. Men were much more likely to be stopped and questioned than women. Anne-Marie was one of about 50 brave women sent as secret agents from the United Kingdom to France.

SOE recruits had to be examined to make sure they were suited to this daring and dangerous life. Over four days, they were given a series of exercises that tested their bravery and intelligence. Many failed these tests, but not Anne-Marie. Her report said that she had "ample courage, determination and a sense of humor."

After this, Anne-Marie went to a special training school in Scotland. Here she learned how to find her way across unknown country and how to send messages by radio or Morse code. She was also taught how to use weapons and ammunitions, as well as how to fight with her bare hands. Later on, Anne-Marie was sent for parachute training. Now all she had to do was wait for the order to go into action.

At last, on December 16, 1943, the call came. Anne-Marie was to parachute into southwest France with another agent. That night, they boarded the aircraft and took off. But it was too foggy to see clearly, and they were forced to turn back. The plane crash-landed, killing four members of the crew.

They made another attempt on January 3, 1944. This time it was a bright, moonlit night. Anne-Marie jumped out of the aircraft, but at first her parachute would not open properly. She tugged and kicked until it was fully open, then floated down into a marshy field.

She later wrote:

There, under my hand lay the soil of France, soft and friendly.

Suddenly, Anne-Marie heard voices nearby. She crouched down in terror. Then she realized they were French voices, so she got up and waved. Members of the Resistance had come to welcome her. Soon, she was safe and warm in a local farmhouse.

The next day, Anne-Marie was driven to a town in the Gascon region of France. As she walked through the streets, she felt very nervous. She thought everyone was looking at her and knew she was a British agent, though of course, they didn't. She told herself she was alone and would have to take care of herself. Anne-Marie was just 20 years old.

That afternoon, she met her commanding officer for the first time. George Starr was a short, bald, and nervous man known as "Le Patron," or the Boss. He was in charge of a huge network of Resistance groups in southwest France and was one of the most successful of all SOE agents.

Starr arranged for Anne-Marie to live at a remote farm in Gascony. She had a new identity as a student from Paris. She even had a new name—Paulette. At the farm, Anne-Marie was looked after by Odilla and Henri Castagnos. She became part of their family, enjoying huge meals, a warm bed, and security. The farmhouse would be a trusty refuge in the terrifying months to come.

By this time, the war was turning in favor of the Allies. They had begun pushing

German and Italian forces out of their conquered territories. The next big event was to be a huge Allied invasion of France due sometime in 1944. The task of the SOE was to help the French Resistance prepare its own uprising once the invasion had started. This meant gathering guns and ammunitions and planning strikes against the Nazis.

Anne-Marie's main job was to carry messages, money, and important papers between the various groups in the network. She had a huge area to cover. It stretched for over 200 miles (320 kilometers), from the Dordogne region down to the Pyrenees on the Spanish border. She traveled by bicycle, bus, and train and even learned to drive vehicles called *gazos*. These were powered by charcoal, since only Germans were allowed to have gasoline.

On her travels, Anne-Marie met all sorts of people. She soon learned whom to fear. German soldiers were easy to spot because of their uniforms. Members of the Gestapo— the dreaded Nazi secret police—were dressed in suits and gray raincoats. Many had close-cropped hair and wore dark glasses. Some French people worked for the German occupiers and were happy to betray their fellow countrymen.

Anne-Marie also learned whom to trust, but only once she knew them well. Among these were her many contacts in the Resistance, including the Castagnos family and their friends. One unexpected ally was the local bus driver. He always kept a warm seat for her at the front and allowed her to get off the bus early to avoid checks by the Gestapo.

Anne-Marie soon found she had other duties. Starr arrived at the farm with news that a group of prisoners had broken out of jail. They were mostly Resistance fighters and SOE agents. Fifteen of them would be arriving in the region. Anne-Marie was to hide them from the Germans and arrange their escape over the border into Spain.

The risks were high. Anne-Marie discovered that the prisoners would have a delay of two weeks before the guides could take them over the mountains. They would also have to pass through the town of Agen, but the Germans had already sent SS (security force) soldiers there. They were setting up roadblocks on all routes out of Agen.

Anne-Marie was jammed in the back of a *gazo* van with the prisoners. The van passed through the first roadblock easily. Then it was stopped at another barrier by policemen who wanted to inspect the cargo. Sensing disaster, the driver put his foot down and roared off. The police yelled "Stop!" and fired a few shots, but the van got away.

On the next day, a much more powerful truck was found to take the prisoners to the foot of the Pyrenees mountain range between France and Spain. Anne-Marie went with them, but it was another nightmare journey. The brakes on the truck did not work properly, making it swerve all over the road. On top of this, the driver brought a box of grenades, which bounced around alarmingly as the truck bumped along. In the end, the prisoners were safely delivered.

In early March 1944, Starr had another refugee for Anne-Marie. His name was Pierre and he was a French police officer who worked for the Resistance in Paris. Pierre was being chased by the Gestapo and needed to escape to Spain. He was carrying a fake identity card and a gun.

The pair boarded a train heading for the Pyrenees. Suddenly, a Gestapo officer entered their cabin and asked to see their documents. He studied Pierre's card for a long time. Anne-Marie felt a chill run down her back. What if he found the gun? Then the German handed back the card, stared at her, and walked out.

Anne-Marie closed her eyes in relief. But Pierre said, "Don't move!" He pulled out his revolver and dropped it behind the seat. At that moment, a figure walked slowly past, giving them a quick look. Then a third man in a raincoat walked by. Pierre explained it was a Gestapo trick to catch suspects unaware. Luckily, they were left alone after that.

There was an even scarier moment a few weeks later. Anne-Marie and a colleague named Claude were waiting to board a train. They were carrying two suitcases filled with guns and ammunitions for the Resistance.

Anne-Marie noticed four Germans on the opposite platform. They were arresting all the men who arrived and taking them away for questioning.

Luckily, the agents got safely onto their train. It was so crowded that Claude had to stand in the aisle with his suitcase. Anne-Marie put the other suitcase on a rack behind her. Then came the dreaded command, "Papers!" A Gestapo officer was questioning Claude, not noticing the suitcase by his legs.

He came to Anne-Marie and asked for her name, address, birthplace, and other details. She recited the fake information she had carefully learned. Satisfied, the man moved away. They were safe!

Suddenly, another officer shouted, "Now open all cases!" They would be sure to find the guns. It was the end, Anne-Marie thought. But they were saved by a woman in the corner, who had two small children. The woman complained that she could not open her suitcases unless the officers cared for her babies for a moment. Embarrassed, the Gestapo men took a quick glance at two other pieces of luggage and left.

Anne-Marie had more lucky escapes in the following weeks. Once, Starr sent her to Paris to pass on important information to another network leader and his radio operator. While waiting to meet her contact, she was surprised to bump into one of her colleagues from the south. He had been sent to warn Anne-Marie that the Germans had captured the radio operator. Now they had set a trap to catch anyone who visited him.

Back in Gascony, Anne-Marie began to feel restless. When would the Allies invade France? Like other members of the Resistance, she longed for this moment. But the invasion was postponed several times. Until then, she would have to continue living in fear and in secret. Anne-Marie missed her family and often wondered what had become of them.

But her cozy life at the farm was about to end. On June 6, 1944, George Starr arrived with news—the Allies had landed in Normandy, and the great invasion had begun. He was forming a *maquis*. This was a band of Resistance fighters hiding in the hills, trying to weaken German control in the area. Anne-Marie was to join these guerrilla fighters.

She packed some old clothes, said goodbye to the Castagnos family, and cycled up to the *maquis* headquarters in the remote village of Castelnau.

Dozens of people bustled around, eager for the fighting to begin. But for many days nothing happened, because there were no Germans nearby. Anne-Marie grew bored, because her main tasks were typing reports and helping to prepare food.

On June 21, everything changed. Shots were heard in the distance, and soon there came news of a major attack. There were at least 700 German troops advancing against the 150 untrained and poorly armed guerrillas. It was time to evacuate the village. Anne-Marie was told to take charge of the security records of the *maquis*. They had to be kept from falling into German hands.

She picked up a machine gun and ran outside. Many people had already left, and there were ear-splitting bangs as mortar shells landed. Where could she hide the papers? Digging a hole, Anne-Marie shoved them inside and covered them with rocks and branches. The Germans never found them, and they were recovered by the *maquis* a few days later.

Anne-Marie and two colleagues jumped into one of the last cars left. As they screeched out of the village, she could see the Germans as small figures in the distance firing at them. When they reached safety, they got out and looked back. Just then, a huge explosion split the air and a cloud of black smoke towered over Castelnau. The last of the *maquis* had blown up the remaining weapons to prevent the Germans from taking them.

By the evening, the Germans had completely destroyed Castelnau. Yet the Resistance fighters felt proud of their battle. They had killed 248 of the enemy and lost only 19 themselves. Most had escaped to fight another day. Anne-Marie was exhausted, but she still helped to tend to the wounded. Then she ate an evening meal with the others—the first food they had eaten all day.

A few weeks after the battle, Starr summoned Anne-Marie. "You must go off to England," he said. There was a large and important document she had to deliver to London, so she would have to climb over the mountains to Spain and then get a boat. This was a terrible blow, because Anne-Marie was desperate to stay in France until the Germans were driven out. Now she would miss it all.

She would also miss her friends and colleagues in Gascony. Fellow Resistance fighters came to say goodbye. Some gave her shoes to wear on her walk or fresh clothes, because Anne-Marie had worn out most of her old ones. One man gave her his last bar of chocolate. Saddest of all, she was unable to see the Castagnos family for a final time because the farm was too far away.

Anne-Marie set out on August 1, 1944. With her were five escaping Allied servicemen and two guides to lead them over the Pyrenees. It was a long and hard journey uphill on a hot day. At first, they all joked and talked, but after an hour they were breathless and silent. On the crest, Anne-Marie looked back at the French landscape she knew so well. She could not stop herself from crying.

Two hours later, they got lost and had to wait for the guides to find the trail. They crept past a German garrison and continued walking until midnight. After a rest, the party continued down the mountainside. By now, they were all exhausted and the guides had left to go home. On and on they trudged, until that evening they saw a village in the distance. An old woman passed them. "Is this Spain?" asked Anne-Marie. The old woman nodded. They were safe at last.

Anne-Marie eventually got back to London in September 1944. She went to SOE headquarters, where she was interviewed about her experiences and wrote a detailed report on the activities of Starr's Resistance network. The end of her service as a secret agent came when she resigned from the SOE in November. World War II in Europe was over six months later, when Germany surrendered on May 8, 1945.

The French government awarded Anne-Marie two medals for her heroic work in the Resistance, including the prized Croix de

Guerre (Cross of War). In 1946, she published a thrilling account of her adventures in a book called *Moondrop to Gascony*. This won the John Llewellyn Rhys Prize, a major literary award.

Anne-Marie went back to France that same year and married Jean-Claude Comert, her childhood sweetheart from school in Geneva. They had a son and a daughter. Anne-Marie spent most of the rest of her life in France and Spain, working as an author and translator. One of her proudest achievements was to buy and restore one of the ruined houses in Castelnau. Anne-Marie died in 1998, at age 75.

Nancy Love:
Ferry Pilot

Restless, beautiful, and adventurous, Nancy
Love was hooked on flying from the age of
16. By her early twenties, she was one of the
top American female pilots. Then, when the
United States entered World War II in 1941,
Nancy founded a group of female pilots who
took on the important job of ferrying combat
aircraft from factories to air bases. Nancy
herself flew almost every type of plane, from
express fighters to enormous bombers such as
the B-17 Flying Fortress.

Nancy was born in Houghton, Michigan,
in 1914. Her father was a wealthy doctor
and could afford to send her to the best local

private schools and buy her nice clothes and good horses. One day in August 1930, Nancy was out riding when she saw a plane taking off from a nearby airfield. Its wings glittered in the sun. She was captivated by the sight.

Nancy—then just 16 years old—rushed to the airfield to find that the pilot was giving flights to anyone who could pay. She paid and went up with him for a trip around the airfield. Then she paid again and went for a longer flight with rolls and loops. Many people would have been frightened or made sick by these stunts, but not Nancy. As soon as they were down, she paid for a third flight. She had found the one thing in life she wanted to do—fly.

That evening, Nancy told her parents about her experience and asked if she could take flying lessons. Her mother disapproved, fearing the lessons would get in the way of her schoolwork, but her father agreed to pay. He said if she wanted to be a pilot, she must "do it well or not at all." Nancy remembered this advice all her life.

A few days later, Nancy went up for her first flying lesson. Her instructor was only 18 and had not been a pilot very long. In those days, there were few rules about qualifications or air safety. After less than five hours in the air, Nancy was allowed to go solo, taking control of the plane herself. By November 1930, she had passed all the tests required to get her private pilot's license.

From then on, flying was her life. In college, Nancy spent all her spare time in the air, gaining experience and learning from her mistakes. Once her plane crashed into a tree and landed upside down. Not realizing this, Nancy unfastened her seat belt and fell to the ground, landing on a stone wall.

After finishing college in 1934, Nancy became a member of the Ninety-Nines, a club exclusively for women pilots founded by the great American aviator Amelia Earhart. Then she met her future husband, Bob Love, who ran his own air travel company. They were married in 1936, and she joined his team of pilots. Nancy also became a test pilot, flying newly developed types of aircraft to check their safety.

In September 1939, the Germans marched into Poland, and World War II began. The British urgently needed to expand their armed forces, especially the Royal Air Force (RAF), to counter the threat of bombing raids and possible invasion. Hundreds of new aircraft had to be developed and built, but who was going to fly them? All available experienced pilots were enlisted, and many more were trained for combat flying.

Pilots were also needed for non-fighting roles such as transporting mail, medical supplies, and other equipment. Another important support task was flying brand-new aircraft from the factories to air bases. But there were not enough men to do the job. So, in January 1940, eight female pilots were recruited to take on these ferrying missions. They were the first British women ever to fly military aircraft regularly.

At this stage, the U.S. government had not joined the war. Even so, many American pilots had gone to the United Kingdom to fly for the RAF, and the United States was supplying aircraft and other equipment to the Allies in Europe. Nancy saw this as a great opportunity. In May 1940, she got in touch with Lieutenant Colonel Robert Olds, of the U.S. Air Corps, suggesting he use women to ferry aircraft for the Army. Nancy even sent him a list of qualified female pilots.

Nancy's proposal was turned down. Olds's commander felt there was no need to use women pilots, believing there were plenty of men available. Nancy went back to her job at Bob's aviation company. But she did get to ferry one plane. This was one of 33 small aircraft that were flown in 1940 to the Canadian border, from where local pilots took them across the Atlantic to France.

The United States entered the war on December 8, 1941, a day after Japanese planes attacked the U.S. fleet at Pearl Harbor in Hawaii. The U.S. government poured money into a massive expansion of the aircraft industry. Over the next two years, U.S. factories produced more than 130,000 warplanes. All of these had to be ferried over long distances from the factories to bases in the United States, Europe, and the Pacific.

Then came a stroke of luck. Bob Love had joined the Air Force and, in 1942, he was sent to defense headquarters in Washington, D.C. Nancy, of course, went with him. She soon got an office job with the Air Transport Command in Baltimore, Maryland. Naturally, Nancy flew the short journey there and back every day in her own small aircraft.

Bob Love casually mentioned his wife's flying skills to a colleague in Washington. This was Colonel Bill Tunner, who was very impressed. At that period, Tunner was searching desperately for skilled ferry pilots. He talked with Nancy, who suggested he should use a squadron of women. She told him she knew of 100 female pilots with the right experience and qualifications.

Tunner asked Nancy to write out a detailed proposal for her idea. In September 1942, this was officially approved. A team of female ferry pilots would be formed called the Women's Auxiliary Ferry Squadron (WAFS). It would not be a military unit, but a civilian one, with Nancy as its commander. The WAFS would be stationed at a new air base in Wilmington, Delaware.

At last, Nancy could begin the task of recruiting female fliers and planning how to train and organize them. The women chosen would have to meet tough standards. They had to have 500 hours of flying time, a commercial pilot's license, and a high school diploma. They also had to be between the ages of 21 and 35 and hold U.S. citizenship.

Soon the first batch of WAFS fliers began arriving. Among them was Betty Gillies, an old friend of Nancy's, who became her second-in-command. Betty had been a pilot since the 1920s. She had even insisted on flying when she was pregnant with her three children, which eventually forced a change in the regulations. Betty was so short that she had to put special blocks on the pedal controls so her feet could reach them.

The recruits lived in their own private quarters in the Wilmington air base. It had housed men before, so it had to be refitted for women. WAFS members had their own special uniforms—blouses, gray-green colored skirts and jackets with brass buttons, and brown leather shoes. When on ferrying duty, the women wore khaki overalls, white silk scarves, and leather flying jackets, along with their goggles and parachutes.

The WAFS' ferrying work began in October 1942. The new recruits flew small single-engine planes from Pennsylvania to Long Island, New York. They discovered it could be long and lonely work, especially when bad weather forced them to make safety stops overnight. In January 1943, the first WAFS group was complete. It contained just under 30 women, who became known as the Originals.

The launch of an all-female squadron was big news. Most male reporters refused to take them seriously. To them, the idea of women flying warplanes was a joke. "What will they think of next?" asked one reporter. Crowds of newsmen came to Wilmington in search of interviews and photographs, especially ones showing the girls' legs, shoulders, or flashing smiles. Nancy warned her new recruits to never cause a bit of scandal and to always be careful how they behaved in public.

The military chiefs quickly realized that the WAFS was a massive success. The demand for pilots continued to grow, and many more women qualified to join the new force. By the summer of 1943, Nancy was in charge of four entire squadrons, based in Texas, Michigan, and California as well as Delaware.

Nancy was thrilled that her plans had worked out so well for the U.S. war effort. She was calm, clever, ambitious, and a good organizer. But she did not want to spend her time on the ground, sitting behind a desk and commanding other people. Her burning ambition was the same as it had been when she was just 16 years old. Nancy wanted to be up in the sky at the controls of a plane.

Flying gave an adventurous person like Nancy two gifts—freedom and power. These were things that women rarely enjoyed during this period, when few jobs or leadership opportunities were open to them. Louise Thaden, one of the great female aviators of the 1930s, wrote:

> Flying is the only real freedom we [women] are privileged to possess.

To gain this freedom, WAFS pilots had to understand and control a complex piece of machinery.

Nancy was eager to fly bigger and faster aircraft, pushing the limits of what female pilots could handle. In February 1943, she tackled the P-51 Mustang. This was the fastest single-engine fighter plane in the U.S. Air Force and, at that time, one of the quickest in the world. Nancy climbed into the Mustang's tiny cockpit and listened to last-minute advice from an instructor. Then she took off and flew for an hour before landing. She described her solo flight as "lonely but wonderful."

Despite Nancy's exploits, the opportunities for women pilots were still very restricted. In March 1943, the male commander of the Ferrying Division of the Air Force published a tough new set of rules. These rules banned women from being copilots with men on flights in bombers and from learning to fly high-powered single-engine planes. This meant that most women could only ever fly in light trainer aircraft.

Nancy immediately objected to these rules, which she thought were unfair. Her arguments were so powerful that, just a month later, some of the limitations were lifted. Most important of all, women pilots were now allowed to gain experience and confidence by flying more powerful aircraft. This gave women the chance to make progress and work their way up to the highest levels of skill.

Another change came in August 1943. It was decided to merge the WAFS with another all-female body that dealt with pilot training. This bigger organization was the Women Airforce Service Pilots, which soon became known as the WASP. Nancy was appointed as Executive for all the WASP ferrying missions.

Summer also brought a huge disappointment for Nancy. She and Betty Gillies had been assigned to ferry the biggest aircraft in the U.S. fleet—the B-17 heavy bomber. With its four engines, 103-foot (31-meter) wingspan, and 13 machine guns, the bomber was known as the Flying Fortress. A large number of B-17s were urgently required in Europe, and pilots were needed to fly them across the Atlantic Ocean.

During July and August 1943, Nancy and Betty prepared for their epic flight. They were rigorously trained in all aspects of controlling the monster plane. They practiced taking off and landing many times and experienced flying both day and night. Operating the heavy Fortress, with its four engines, required strength and endurance, but the women worked tirelessly and were officially approved as competent crew for the B-17.

On September 5, the two women and their crew were in Labrador, in northeastern Canada, preparing their aircraft for the long journey over the Atlantic. But, as they sat at dinner, a telegram arrived from the Air Force commander, General "Hap" Arnold. He had only just been told about the flight and was horrified. Women, he believed, should not be flying a military plane into a war zone. Nancy and Betty must be replaced by men.

Their dream was shattered, but they had to obey orders. The next day, they posed for photographers in front of their B-17 as they waited for the replacements to arrive. Their male colleagues had tried to cheer them up by painting the name "Queen Bee" on the plane during the night, but it was a very small victory. While the Flying Fortress set off for the United Kingdom, Nancy and Betty were sent back home, feeling angry and humiliated.

Nancy now worked even harder, to cover up her frustration. The use of women to ferry planes grew into a major success under her command, and eventually her four squadrons employed 180 pilots. By December 1944, WASP fliers had delivered 12,650 aircraft across the United States in just over two years. These included more than 70 different types of plane, most of them high-speed, single-engine fighters.

By this time, the Allies were definitely on the way to winning the war. U.S. military expansion had reached its peak, and so many male pilots had been trained that there was no longer any shortage. It was decided that men could now do all the ferrying of aircraft. The female pilots were no longer needed and, on October 1, 1944, General Arnold announced that the WASP would be disbanded.

Nancy's last trip as a ferry pilot took place on December 15, 1944. She flew a four-engine transport aircraft from Chicago to the West Coast. On December 19, Nancy sat down to a farewell dinner in Wilmington, with many of her WASP colleagues. Among them were eight of the Originals, including Betty Gillies. After that, there was nothing else to do but pack up and leave, putting an end to the WASP.

But Nancy would have one more airborne adventure. On December 27, she set out on an official expedition to Asia to inspect military supply routes from India to China.

This involved flying over the massive mountain ranges of the Himalayas, known to American pilots as the Hump. Nancy herself took the controls for part of the flight from Calcutta to Kunming in China. She was the first female American pilot to fly the Hump.

When the war finished in 1945, Nancy was awarded an Air Medal for her wartime service to the United States. She and Bob both became civilians again and settled in Martha's Vineyard, Massachusetts, with their three daughters. But the women Nancy had flown with remained her closest friends, and many of them came to visit for summer vacations. Nancy still had a small plane and enjoyed flying by herself from an airfield next to their house. She died in 1976, at age 62.

In 2010, the U.S. government awarded Nancy's WASPs the Congressional Gold Medal—the highest award Congress can present to civilians.

Ruby Loftus:
Gunmaker

Ruby Loftus was a shy girl with no great ambitions. She might have led an unexciting, ordinary life had it not been for World War II. Ruby went to work in a weapons factory in Wales, in the United Kingdom, where she discovered she had a special talent. She was a superb machine operator, trusted with the task of making important gun parts. Ruby also found fame when a portrait was painted of her at work. It became an iconic image of women's contribution to the war effort.

Ruby was born in Newport, Wales, in 1921, the second of four children. With her parents, her two sisters (Elsie and Queenie), and her brother, Harold, Ruby then lived in the little town of Llanhilleth, Wales. But times were hard. During the early 1930s, the United Kingdom and Europe were in an economic depression and work was difficult to find. The Loftus family moved to London, England, where there was more chance of finding work.

They settled in north London, and Ruby's father worked for a gasoline company. Soon, Ruby herself left school and also found her very first job. She worked as an assistant in a tobacco shop near her home. It was here that she first met John Green, the young man who would later become her husband.

Ruby might have settled down to a quiet and happy life. But then tragedy struck. First, in 1938, her father died suddenly. Not only was this heartbreaking for the family, but it also robbed them of their main money earner. Then, in September 1939, came the outbreak of World War II. Within a year, London had become a major target of heavy German bombing, known as the Blitz.

In 1940, Ruby's mother, Martha, decided it would be safer for the family to move out of London and back to Newport, in Wales. The only house she could afford there was a small apartment above a store near a chemical factory. Everyone had to find work as soon as possible. Martha took a job as a porter at the Newport railroad station, while Ruby's brother, Harold, joined the Royal Navy.

The three Loftus sisters applied for jobs at the Royal Ordnance Factory (ROF) in Newport in November 1940. The factory had just been built near their home to manufacture guns for the British Army and Navy. Competition for jobs was fierce. Of the 120 women who applied, only 75 were selected. Elsie, Ruby, and Queenie were among them.

This success made a huge difference in their lives. Not only was everyone in the family now earning money, they were also able to move into a bigger and better house. People who got jobs at the ROF were officially in reserved occupations, or jobs that were important to the war effort. This meant that the family was allowed to move into one of the new houses built in the area for these workers.

During this time, the country was in desperate need of firearms, ammunition, aircraft, and other military equipment. The British government had begun encouraging women to work in the weapons industry.

They had to fill the places left empty by the enormous numbers of men joining the armed forces or working in civil defense. Many of these men had been skilled engineers who had many years of training and experience. Somehow, they had to be replaced—as quickly as possible.

Ruby and her sisters began their basic training, which lasted for a year. They joined other women who had previously worked in many different kinds of jobs. These women had worked as waitresses, store clerks, warehouse workers, domestic workers, barmaids, and nurses. One woman had even been a professional dancer. All of these women had to learn entirely new and unfamiliar skills in a special school set up in the factory.

First, they were taught basic techniques, including how to use simple engineering tools, how to measure accurately, and how to read technical drawings. After this, the women took a test, which everyone had to pass. This made them more confident when they moved onto the floor of the factory itself, where the lathes, mills, and other machines were operated. They each set to work at a machine, guided by skilled men.

Some machines at the factory were simpler to operate than others. They had special tools and guides, which they could use to do their work accurately and quickly. But other machines were harder. It was not easy to use a lathe. These machines were used to make weapon parts that had to be cut to exact measurements so they fit together perfectly.

The Newport ROF manufactured two types of weapon. The first was the Bofors gun. This was a heavy, quick-firing gun used by the armed forces of the United Kingdom and (later) the United States. It became one of the most important and effective weapons of the war, especially against enemy aircraft. The second was a big gun used against tanks.

Making these weapons was a long and complex process, with many different operations. The factory managers had to find a way for this to be done by barely trained workers. They broke down each operation into a number of much smaller sections—as many as eight or ten. This way, the workers had simpler and shorter tasks to perform.

Even so, making parts for the Bofors and the antitank guns demanded a high level of skill. The heart of the weapon was the breech ring, which sat right behind the gun barrel and took the greatest pressure. The trickiest operation was cutting the screw threads on this ring. If these were not made properly, the gun might explode when it was fired. So, the operator's hands and eyes had to work perfectly together to make sure there was no mistake. The cutting had to be precisely correct to within 0.002 inch (0.05 millimeter). That's the width of a human hair!

Many of the male workers at the factory did not think women could be trained so quickly to do the jobs of skilled men. In fact, some believed women workers would never be able to do men's work properly. But they were soon proven wrong. During World War II, women showed that they could do top-quality work, disproving the idea that engineering was just a man's job.

At Newport, Ruby was a shining example. She became an outstanding machinist in an amazingly short time. The manager of the Ordnance Factory noted:

> Whatever we gave her to do, she did, and did perfectly.

In just seven months, Ruby mastered the most difficult job in the factory—the screwing of the breech ring. Before this, only a male worker with eight or nine years of training would have been allowed to tackle the task.

Ruby was so good that other people in the factory came to admire her workmanship, almost as if it were a work of art. The older skilled men in the machine shop had started by rejecting the idea of women machinists. Now they were amazed.

The sudden arrival of Ruby and her colleagues was a shock for the factory managers. They had to provide extra facilities for their female workers, such as separate restrooms as well as nurseries for those with young children. At Newport, there was a Lady Welfare Supervisor who tended to the women's needs. There was also a first aid station, staffed by four nurses, and a doctor who visited every morning. A dentist, an eye doctor, a masseur, and even a hairdresser were also available.

The workers ate in a large hall. Most of the vegetables served were grown on the factory grounds, where pigs and hens were kept to provide fresh meat and eggs.

Concerts and dances were also held in the cafeteria. There was plenty to do on days off. Men and women had their own teams for sports such as soccer, hockey, and tennis. There was even an indoor rifle club. The members lay on the floor, rested their guns on sandbags, and shot at targets at the end of a long hallway.

Despite this, Ruby soon discovered that life in the factory was not much fun. The workforce was split into two 12-hour shifts. The day shift worked from 8 a.m. to 8 p.m., and the night shift from 8 p.m. to 8 a.m. In this way, the factory stayed in operation without stopping throughout the week. Workers were regularly switched from one shift to another. Many found this very hard, especially at night, when they felt sleepy and confused.

There was very little variety in the work. Performing the same small operation time after time throughout a long shift could be very boring. The only big break was one hour at lunchtime, when the workers went to the cafeteria for a meal. Later, tea was brought to the women as they worked. To make things worse, the factory was very noisy and dark, even during the day. There were no windows at all, because any light coming from the building could have attracted enemy bombers.

The machine room was a dangerous place, too. Not only was it dark, but it was also slippery because of machine oil spilled on the floor. Then there were the machines themselves. In spite of safety guards, several workers were badly injured when their fingers or hair got trapped in moving parts. Fragments of metal from the lathes could also get embedded in their hands, making them very sore.

Ruby's life was about to change. She was already a star performer at the factory, but in 1943, she became a national celebrity. The story began in January, when the manager sent for her. He told Ruby that the most famous female artist in the United Kingdom, Laura Knight, was coming to paint a picture of her while she worked.

Laura Knight was one of many artists employed by the government during World War II. She was commissioned to produce paintings of suitable subjects as a record of wartime life. Laura had already painted members of the Women's Auxiliary Air Force (WAAF) and had been asked to make a picture to honor the work of women in munitions factories. Ruby had been chosen because of her outstanding skill and because she was so young, being just 21 years old.

Laura arrived in March. She met Ruby, who was wearing blue jeans, a pink blouse, and a green hairnet. Laura said how nice the colors looked and asked her to wear the same combination while she was being painted. She watched Ruby at work and made rough sketches. At the end of the first day, Laura chose the best of the sketches as the basis for the picture.

The following morning, Laura set up her easel with its bare canvas on the factory floor, with a low partition to shield her from trucks and other equipment going past. She was not at all disturbed by the noise and bustle of work going on around her. By the end of the day, she had sketched out the rough outlines of the picture. In all this time, Ruby continued with her normal work at the lathe, cutting screws for the breech rings of the antitank guns.

Over the next three weeks, Laura slowly built up the picture using oil paints. She worked hard all day, from early in the morning. In fact, Laura grew so absorbed in her painting that she often forgot to eat or drink. A factory employee had to take her by the arm to get up and have a cup of tea.

Laura did not seem worried by the dangers in the machine shop, with heavy weapons parts being carried by cranes far above her head. One day, a gun wheel came loose and crashed down toward her. She did not jump back out of the way, but rather fell forward over the canvas to protect it. The wheel smashed to the floor, just missing her.

At last, the painting was nearly complete. Laura took it back to her studio to make the final touches and get it ready to go on display at the Summer Exhibition at London's Royal Academy in April 1943. Ruby made arrangements to go to the opening of the exhibition.

But then she had another big surprise. A newsreel company wanted to make a film of Ruby and Laura at the Royal Academy. Ruby would have to go to London two days early. On the morning of April 29, Ruby set off by car with four other factory workers. At the Royal Academy, she and Laura were filmed shaking hands and looking at the painting.

The next day was even more exciting. Art critics had their first glimpse of the painting, called simply *Ruby Loftus Screwing a Breech-Ring*, and voted it Picture of the Year.

Journalists from newspapers and radio lined up to interview Ruby. Photographs of her soon appeared on front pages all over the country. One evening, she was taken to a special cocktail party at the Ritz Hotel, where she met many famous people. This was all quite a shock for the shy girl from Wales, who said:

Altogether it was rather frightening, until I got used to it.

The year 1943 held yet another major event for Ruby. That September, she married John Green, the man she had met all those years ago in London. He had spent the war as a soldier, fighting in the struggle against the Germans in North Africa. After this, Ruby's life went back to normal. She returned to Newport and her lathe in the factory.

But she had a proud place in the history of World War II. Long before the age of television and social media, Laura Knight's painting of her became a popular image of how women proved themselves to be equal to men in a difficult environment. It was reproduced as a print and a poster and is still known all over the world today. Ruby had her own special reminder of that period—one of Laura's original sketches of her.

When the war ended in 1945, Ruby was offered the chance to enroll in a full-time engineering program sponsored by the government. However, she and John had already decided to leave the United Kingdom and settle in Canada. In 1948, they immigrated to British Columbia, where they spent the rest of their lives. Ruby died in 2004, at age 83.

Red Harrington:
Navy Nurse and
Prisoner of War

Mary Rose "Red" Harrington was a U.S. Navy nurse in the Pacific during World War II. In 1941, she was one of many nurses captured when the Japanese invaded the Philippines. They were held in prison camps for over three years in harsh conditions, often starving and in constant fear. Even so, Red and her colleagues continued with their heroic work, setting up hospitals and helping the wounded and sick.

Mary Rose had a tough start in life. She was born in 1913 in Sioux City, Iowa, in a home for unmarried mothers. Abandoned by her parents, Mary Rose was sent to live in an orphanage. But very soon, her luck changed. She was spotted by Petra Harrington, a childless woman who came to the orphanage looking for a child to adopt. Something about the calm little baby girl touched Petra. She took Mary Rose home to her farm at Elk Point, South Dakota, where Petra lived with her husband.

Mary Rose Harrington had a happy childhood with her new family in the quiet countryside. There was a pond to skate on in the winter and a river for swimming in the summer. As a teenager, she worked hard in school, but enjoyed herself twice a week at the local dance hall. Because of her hair color, Mary Rose soon got the nickname Red, which stuck with her for the rest of her life.

Petra Harrington taught her daughter to be independent and rely on her own strength of character. When Red left high school, her big ambition was to be a journalist. But this was the early 1930s, when an economic depression swept across the United States. Newspaper jobs were drying up, so Red decided to train as a nurse instead. She graduated from nursing school in Sioux City in 1934.

Private nursing conditions in those days were hard, and salaries were miserable. Red's wages actually dropped to only $4 for a 20-hour day, so she barely had enough money for food. Worse still, her father died, leaving Red to support her mother. Looking for a better job, Red turned to the U.S. Navy. In January 1937, she joined the Navy Nurse Corps training hospital in San Diego, California. Her mother moved in nearby, happy to live in warm, sunny California.

Red enjoyed military life and progressed well at the hospital. Being a Navy nurse gave her exciting opportunities to work overseas, and she soon applied for a job at a U.S. naval base far away in the Philippines. In January 1941, she said goodbye to Petra and boarded a military transport ship heading west across the Pacific.

The United States had controlled the Philippines since the start of the century. The islands were a major center of U.S. military power in the Western Pacific region. This was seen as an important counter to the threat from Japan, which had already invaded China and was expanding its empire in other parts of Southeast Asia.

After a 30-day voyage, Red arrived in Manila, the capital of the Philippines, on the island of Luzon. She went to work at the Cañacao Naval Hospital, near the massive Cavite shipyard on the shores of Manila Bay. She lived here with 11 other nurses in a grand two-story building with polished floors and verandas overlooking the bay. Red loved her new job, working an eight-hour day with plenty of weekends off.

But she loved the fun-filled social life of the Filipino capital even more. For American servicemen and women, Manila was a paradise, the hot days and warm nights filled with the scent of exotic flowers. There were many ways to have fun, from golf, swimming, and tennis to cocktail parties, dances, and boat trips to nearby islands. Cooks, maids, gardeners, and tailors tended to their daily needs. The war seemed a long way away.

But the lazy days on Luzon were about to end. On December 7, 1941, Japanese warplanes made a surprise attack on the U.S. naval base at Pearl Harbor, in the Hawaiian Islands. They wrecked the Pacific fleet, destroying 188 aircraft and killing over 2,200 Americans. U.S. naval power in the region was crippled. The United States, stunned by the assault, declared war on Japan.

Red Harrington was on duty in Cañacao Naval Hospital early the next morning when the terrible news reached the Philippines. All at once, she heard shouting outside. An American sailor ran into the ward, yelling that Honolulu had been bombed. At first, Red could not understand what he meant. But that very same day, Japanese aircraft arrived in the Philippines.

Their bombs rained down on a U.S. Army base north of Manila. Another wave of warplanes hit Clark Field, the major U.S. Air Force base, dropping bombs and sweeping the field with gunfire. Within a few hours, the bases were littered with mangled aircraft and blazing buildings. U.S. air power in the Philippines had been destroyed. The enemy now controlled the sky and the sea.

The attacks went on day after day. By December 14, the Cavite shipyard and the Cañacao naval base had been smashed to rubble and much of the city was on fire. On December 22, a large Japanese invasion army landed on the north side of Luzon and began its march toward Manila. U.S. commanders abandoned the city and retreated with most of their forces to the narrow peninsula of Bataan and the island of Corregidor, on the west side of Manila Bay.

Red Harrington and the rest of the Navy nurses were among those left behind. Cañacao hospital had been badly damaged, so the Navy took over a nearby school to house the huge number of people wounded in the bombings. The nurses and doctors had to work around the clock to tend to their patients, many of whom were too badly hurt to be moved.

Just after Christmas, Red and her colleagues were told to get ready to leave Manila. Then nothing happened. Everyone else seemed to be fleeing, but not the Navy nurses. Red asked her chief nurse, Laura Cobb, what was happening. She was told they had no orders to leave, so they had to stay put.

By December 31, the invaders had reached the outskirts of Manila. At the school, the nurses watched as the U.S. flag was lowered, then burned, so it could not fall into enemy hands. Two days later, Japanese troops arrived to take over the city. The hospital workers surrendered. The Japanese took everything valuable from the buildings, but the nurses' rooms were untouched.

Those who remained were now prisoners of war, with little control over their lives. Barbed wire was placed around the buildings. The Japanese soldiers bullied the sick and injured, forcing many of them to get out of their beds and join working parties. One night, four patients escaped. The soldiers threatened that the next time this happened, the ward nurse would be shot along with two other patients.

In March 1942, the hospital was closed down. The male patients, along with doctors and other American servicemen, were moved to a prison in the city. One nurse had escaped before the invasion. The 11 remaining nurses were sent to an internment camp at Santo Tomas University, on the other side of Manila.

The university was a grand building, with high stone walls and spacious gardens. But by the time Red Harrington arrived, it was quickly turning into a cramped and crowded prison camp. By July, over 3,800 people were held captive there—Americans, Britons, Australians, and other foreign nationals. A quarter of them were children, and another quarter were adult women.

Like the other prisoners, the nurses slept in dormitories, with separate quarters for men and women. Beds were shoved together with hardly any space between them. Each nurse was given a plate, a cup, a spoon, and two small meals a day. The food was always the same— watery rice, corn mush, and a few vegetables.

Prisoners could buy more food, as well as other important supplies, if they had money.

There was a camp store, and Filipino traders came in every day to sell fruits, vegetables, eggs, and cigarettes. But their prices were high, and people who ran out of cash had to borrow from those who were richer. Only a few of the prisoners went hungry at this stage, but things would get far worse in the months to come.

Soon Red and her friends were joined by 64 Army nurses. The U.S. and Filipino forces on Bataan had finally surrendered after a long and savage siege. While the captured servicemen had been taken away to brutal military prison camps, the nurses who had been with them were treated as civilians and brought to Santo Tomas.

There was already a small medical center in the camp, but it was not large enough to cope with the arriving flood of wounded and sick people. Together, the nurses arranged for a bigger hospital to be set up in a nearby convent building. By this time, many people coming into camp had deadly diseases that were highly contagious, including dysentery and tuberculosis. These patients were kept in a separate ward.

It was essential for the doctors to know exactly what kind of tropical diseases they were dealing with. Red helped to establish a hospital laboratory, where blood and other body samples from patients could be analyzed. She soon made herself an expert in identifying the bacteria and parasites that carried the infections.

Red was a smart and hardworking nurse with a bright smile. But she also stood out as a feisty young woman who refused to let the misery and fear of prison camp life get her down. And she was willing to put herself in danger in order to help others. Red knew that the doctors and medical officers from Cañacao were locked in Bilibid Prison in Manila, where they had been joined by servicemen captured on Bataan. Starving, cruelly treated, and living in filthy conditions, many were dying.

Red and a few other nurses made contact with Filipino resistance agents, who were secretly working against the Japanese. With their help, the nurses smuggled food and clothes to the men in Bilibid. The nurses were also given money for the prisoners by local Catholic priests. They hid this, along with messages, inside hollowed-out fruits or boxes of medicine sent to the prison.

Meanwhile, the population of the Santo Tomas camp kept growing. By May 1943, there were over 4,100 prisoners, and the Japanese feared overcrowding might cause riots. They decided to establish a new internment camp south of Manila, near a town called Los Baños. It would be set in an old farming school, high up in the tropical rain forest.

This was a chance to move out of the cramped, filthy chaos of Santo Tomas to a cooler location. Over 800 men volunteered to go and build the new camp, but they also needed medical care. Red Harrington saw this as an opportunity for a fresh start and begged her commander, Laura Cobb, to volunteer the Navy nurses as well. Laura quickly got to work, and on the following day the nurses were ordered to pack, ready for the move.

On the morning of May 14, Red and the rest of the volunteers climbed aboard trucks and waved goodbye to their friends. At the nearest railroad station, their nightmare journey began. They were stuffed into steel boxcars with barely enough room to stand, and the doors were slammed shut. The temperature quickly rose. Soaked in sweat and starved of fresh air, the prisoners had to endure an agonizing journey lasting seven hours before they reached Los Baños.

Once again, doctors and nurses set up a prison hospital from scratch out in the jungle. They had buildings but very little equipment or medicine, so they had to improvise. Beds and tables were made from bamboo. Bedpans and basins were made from corrugated tin from the roof. Mosquito netting was woven from banana fibers, and drinking glasses were cut from old beer bottles.

Medicine had to be mixed from local ingredients. Syrup made from onion juice and sugar stopped patients from coughing and spreading their contagious germs. Tea from guava leaves was used to treat dysentery. There were no sticky bandages, so the nurses took sap from rubber trees, mixed it into a paste with oil, and used this to stick bandages in place.

But one big problem remained—there were not enough nurses. There were now only 11 of them to care for over 1,000 prisoners. Laura decided to train up some of the men to work as hospital orderlies and asked Red to take charge of them. Among the volunteers was a civilian named Page Nelson. Soon, he and

Red fell in love. There was no chance of a wedding in a prison camp, but Page gave her a ring. They promised to marry if they survived the war.

However, the war still had a long time to run. Throughout 1944, living conditions for the prisoners at Los Baños grew steadily worse. Many more people arrived at the camp, until it became seriously overcrowded. Without running water or proper drainage, the land and buildings became filthy. Infectious diseases spread quickly, and so did the rats. The Japanese cut down the rations of food, and much of what they provided was rotten and inedible.

By December 1944, an average of one or two prisoners were dying every day in Los Baños. All the rest were suffering from disease or starvation. Lack of fresh food and vitamins caused beriberi, dysentery, and scurvy. Hunger gave people headaches, swollen feet, and feelings of dizziness, leaving them unable to walk. The nurses often found they were so weak they could barely do their work. During the time she was a prisoner, Red Harrington's weight fell from 130 pounds (59 kilograms) to just 95 pounds (43 kilograms).

Meanwhile, the United States and its allies were winning the war in the Pacific. They had destroyed the Japanese fleet and were now within bombing range of Tokyo, Japan's capital. In January 1945, U.S. troops landed on Luzon, where they met fierce resistance.

Progress was slow, so special forces were sent through enemy lines to liberate the prison camps in Manila. They reached Santo

Tomas camp on February 3, freeing the prisoners there. But in Los Baños, the starving continued. All Red and her friends had to eat was 11 ounces (300 grams) of rice a day. It was not until February 22 that salvation arrived.

Early that morning, Red was on duty in the hospital. Hearing the drone of a plane, she looked up and saw a parachute coming down. It was the start of a lightning raid by U.S. troops and Filipino guerrillas. Paratroopers attacked from one side, while infantry broke through the main gate. The 2,000 prisoners and remaining Navy nurses were loaded onto trucks and driven to safety. Their long and terrible ordeal was over.

After a rest period, the Navy nurses were flown back to San Francisco in mid-March. A week after that, Red returned to San Diego and saw her mother for the first time in more than four years. In April, she and Page were reunited when he at last returned from the Philippines. They got married in San Diego as soon as they could, then settled in Virginia.

Red never went back to full-time hospital nursing. She and Page had four children, and she later worked as a volunteer for the Red Cross and in the local school. She rarely talked about her heroic achievements in the war. But the terrible conditions in the prison camps left their mark. If the children brought friends home for dinner, there was one simple rule. Nobody was allowed to leave a scrap of food on their plate!

Mary Rose "Red" Harrington died in 1999, at age 85.

After World War II

Germany surrendered to the Allied forces in May 1945. Fighting in the Pacific continued until September, when the Japanese also surrendered. World War II was over at last. Women had made a huge contribution to the Allied cause. In the United States, there were more than 18 million female war workers by 1945. In the United Kingdom, there were over 6.5 million female civilian war workers.

It did not stay that way. After the war, millions of soldiers returned home from the fighting and needed work. As a result, many women lost their jobs, and the workforce was once again dominated by men. But the experience of work had won women a lot of respect and self-confidence. Things would never be the same as before the war.

Other Important Figures

Idella Purnell (1901–1982)

Idella joined the Woman's Land Army of America in the summer before she was due to go to college. At 17, she was a year too young to join, but she passed the physical entrance test and simply never mentioned her age to anyone! The job of "land girls" like her was to make sure that farms produced as much food as possible while male workers were away fighting. Most of these women had never worked on a farm before, but were needed to do every kind of work, from plowing and harvesting to herding sheep and catching rats.

Mavis Batey (1921–2013)

Mavis was only 19 when she went to work at Bletchley Park in the United Kingdom. Women were a crucial part of the team there. They helped to crack the secret codes used by the Germans in their radio messages. Mavis was a talented code-breaker, and her work played a big part in the Allied victory.

Charity Adams Earley (1918–2002)

Charity was the first African American woman to serve as an officer in the Women's Army Auxiliary Corps. In 1944, she was commander of the first unit of African American women to be sent to Europe. Women in the Corps took on many non-fighting jobs, becoming radio operators, electricians, and air-traffic controllers.

Constance Babington Smith (1912–2000)

Constance worked at a secret Royal Air Force (RAF) station near London. She was an expert at analyzing photographs. During the war, spy planes took thousands of aerial photographs over enemy-held territory. Women were part of the team that carefully examined the photos for valuable information. Constance helped to discover sites in Germany where new types of missiles were being built.

Timeline

1939

September 3   The United Kingdom (UK)
and France declare war on
Germany. World War II begins.

1940

May   Germany invades the Low
Countries and France.

Anne-Marie Walters and her
family move to the UK.

Nancy Love proposes a
squadron of women ferry
pilots. Her idea is rejected.

June 22   France signs a surrender
agreement with Germany.

November   Ruby Loftus applies for a job at
the Royal Ordnance Factory in
Newport, Wales.

1941

Anne-Marie Walters joins the WAAF.

January Red Harrington sails to new nursing post in Manila, Philippines.

December 7 Japanese attack Pearl Harbor.

December 8 The United States (U.S.) and UK declare war on Japan. Japanese begin bombing raids on Luzon, Philippines.

December 15 Japanese ground forces launch invasion of the Philippines.

December 31 U.S. forces in Manila surrender to Japanese.

1942

March Red Harrington and other Navy nurses are sent to prison camp at Santo Tomas, Luzon.

September Nancy Love's idea for women ferry pilots is approved.

October The first WAFS squadron begins ferrying new planes across U.S.

1943

February   Nancy Love becomes the first woman to fly the advanced Mustang fighter plane.

March   Laura Knight begins her portrait of Ruby Loftus at work.

April 30   Laura's painting of Ruby Loftus goes on show at the Royal Academy, London.

May   Red Harrington is sent to a new prison camp at Los Baños, Luzon.

July   Anne-Marie Walters is selected for SOE training. Nancy Love becomes the first woman to fly the B-17 Flying Fortress heavy bomber.

August   The WAFS is reorganized into the WASP.

1944

January 3	Anne-Marie Walters parachutes into southwest France.
June 6	D-Day: Allies launch a massive invasion in Normandy, France.
August 1	Anne-Marie Walters leaves France on her long journey back to the UK.
October 20	U.S. forces land on the Philippines.
December 19	The WASP is disbanded.

1945

January	Nancy Love becomes the first female pilot to fly over the Himalayas. U.S. and Filipino troops land on Luzon.
February 22	Red Harrington and others are liberated from Los Baños.
May 8	Germany surrenders.
August 15	Japan surrenders. World War II ends.

Find Out More

Books

Atwood, Kathryn J. *Women Heroes of World War II: 26 Stories of Espionage, Sabotage, Resistance, and Rescue*. Chicago: Chicago Review Press, 2011.

Farrell, Mary Cronk. *Pure Grit: How American World War II Nurses Survived Battle and Prison Camp in the Pacific*. New York: Abrams, 2014.

Price, Sean. *Rosie the Riveter: Women in World War II* (American History Through Primary Sources). Chicago: Raintree, 2009.

Web sites

Facthound offers a safe, fun way to find Internet sites related to this book. All of the sites on Facthound have been researched by our staff.

Here's all you do:

Visit www.facthound.com

Type in this code: 9781484608654

Glossary

civilian person not in the armed forces

cockpit space for a pilot in a small aircraft

competent having the right skills or qualifications

economic depression time of severe decline, with falling trade, prices, and jobs

garrison military post

guerrilla member of an unofficial band of fighters, trying to overthrow an occupying army

internment imprisonment of a group of non-military people within a country

lathe machine on which a piece of metal or wood is spun around, then shaped or cut by a fixed tool

Morse code system of sending messages in which letters are replaced by patterns of short or long signals

munitions materials for fighting, such as guns or ammunition

newsreel short film about a news event, shown in movie theaters in the 1940s

ordnance guns, ammunition, and bombs

peninsula thin piece of land that sticks out into the sea

resistance organization in a country that struggles to get rid of an occupying army

wingspan space between the two wing tips of an aircraft (or bird)

workforce total number of workers in a country or company

Index